Advanced NFS Techniques

Optimizing Distributed File Systems

Table of Contents

Chapter 1. Introduction

Today's expanding digital world demands more efficient systems for managing, accessing, and storing data. Welcome to our Special Report on "Advanced NFS Techniques: Optimizing Distributed File Systems". Navigate the intricate labyrinth of Network File System (NFS) with this comprehensive report, whether you're a seasoned network administrator or an aspiring one. Our report provides a deep dive into advanced techniques and tools to maximize optimization in distributed file systems. We guarantee a pragmatic and down-to-earth approach, ensuring even the technical aspects are easily digestible. You don't need to be a tech wizard to embrace what lies ahead - let our special report take the complexity out of NFS!

Chapter 2. Understanding the Basics of NFS

To start off, it's essential to understand that Network File System (NFS) is a distributed file system protocol engineered by Sun Microsystems in 1984. The main goal of NFS is to allow client computers to access files over a network in a way that makes it seem as if the files were on their local storage.

2.1. The Basic Functioning of NFS

NFS operates on a client-server model, where an NFS server serves or shares directories and files with its client(s). These served files and directories are mounted on the client machine, allowing them to access the shared data as though it's stored locally on the client machine. Every file and directory shared has a path relative to a root directory. When an NFS client requests a file from the server, the server uses this path to determine what file or directory to provide.

2.2. How NFS Differs

A commendable trait of NFS lies in its ability to provide a common file system over a network that allows a computer to access files in the same manner as local files. Other distinct features that differentiate NFS include:

- Network Operating System Independence: As a protocol, NFS is not eager about the type of network, the operating system, or even the file system each server or client uses. This feature offers great flexibility and adaptability across heterogenous environments.

- Support for Symmetric Multiprocessing (SMP): NFS is an SMP-friendly protocol. In the context of multiple concurrent operations, NFS can access remote files as efficiently as the local operating system accesses local files.

- Statelessness: NFS server does not maintain a connection state, allowing it to recover quickly in the instance of a failure. Its stateless nature lends itself to scalability and resilience in case of server failures and network instabilities.

2.3. NFS Versions

There have been several versions of NFS, each adding improvements and modifications for optimization. The primary versions are NFSv2, NFSv3, and NFSv4.

1. NFSv2: Introduced in 1989, it is a stateless and connectionless protocol. Although older, it is still widely used due to its simplicity and efficiency.

2. NFSv3: Introduced in 1995, added support for 64-bit file sizes and offsets to handle files larger than 2GB. It also introduced a more efficient READDIRPLUS operation.

3. NFSv4: Not just a revision, but a complete rewrite. Launched in 2000, offers stateful and lock operations integrated within the protocol, introduces a pseudo file system and includes internationalization features.

2.4. The NFS Communication Protocol

Communication between the NFS client and server follows a Remote Procedure Call (RPC) model. As an intermediary, RPC translates network communication requests between the client and server. The client sends a request in the form of a procedure call that includes the procedure's parameters. The server, on receiving the call, processes it and sends back the output.

In terms of transport protocols, NFS can be implemented over both TCP (Transmission Control Protocol) and UDP (User Datagram Protocol). While TCP ensures data transmission reliability, the less complex UDP enables faster communications.

2.5. Understanding NFS Architecture

At its core, NFS is designed in layers:

1. The RPC Layer: This is the base layer where NFS client and server communicate. The RPC package builds and sends the calls to the server, and subsequently decodes and interprets the server's response.

2. The XDR Layer: XDR (External Data Representation) is a standard format used by NFS for serializing data. It is responsible for translating data structures defined in the RPC layer so that computers with different architectures can interpret the data uniformly.

3. The NFS Layer: This is where requests for certain files or operations from the client are mapped to operations on the local file system of the server.

2.6. Conclusion

In conclusion, NFS has revolutionized the way networked systems interconnect and share resources. The fundamental understanding of NFS forms the basis for further exploration into advanced techniques and optimizations related to distributed file systems. It is a highly dynamic protocol, designed with flexibility in mind, and is adaptable across diverse system environments. Its continuous evolution to meet the needs of complex, distributed networks has cemented its status as the standard protocol in the realm of distributed file systems. This introduction paints a broad picture of the basic components and functionality of NFS, paving the way to delve deeper into intricate optimizations and advanced implementations.

Chapter 3. Architectural Overview of Distributed File Systems

Distributed File Systems (DFS) lay the foundation for data sharing and storage in multi-computer systems. Peer to peer or client/server systems primarily benefit from such systems owing to its inherent ability of data sharing and redundancy. DFS offer an abstraction of a single integrated namespace where data storage and retrieval are efficient, reliable, and secure.

3.1. Introduction to Distributed File Systems

The inception of distributed file systems introduces a paradigm shift from single-node file systems to multi-node file systems - enabling the concurrent access on multiple machines in the network. For this reason, DFS significantly accelerates data processing in both sequential and random access patterns, enhancing system efficiency. The logical sequence of data in a distributed file system allows applications to access data without considering its physical location. The same mechanism enhances the performance, scalability, and reliability of data handling in distributed tasks.

3.2. Key Components of Distributed File Systems

Distributed File Systems typically comprise four key components: the Client, the Server, Metadata, and Data. When a client seeks a file, it asks the Server over a network. In response, the Server permits the Client to get access to the Data and Metadata associated with the requested file.

Data includes actual file content that the Client seeks, whereas Metadata is the information about the file, such as the location, size, owner, and updates.

3.3. Types of Distributed File Systems

There are primarily two types of DFS: symmetric and asymmetric. Symmetric DFS, also known as peer-to-peer systems, treats all nodes equally in the file processing pipeline. Each node possesses client and server functionalities, sharing resources on an equal footing. Conversely, in Asymmetric DFS or client/server file systems, nodes are split into servers or clients based on the tasks performed. Evidently, servers store and manage file resources, whereas clients engage in requesting and consuming these resources.

3.4. Working of Distributed File Systems

DFS operate through file servers across the network. They receive a request from a client machine and then serve the files to the client. Their working mechanism is further classified into stateless and stateful systems.

In a Stateless DFS, the server does not maintain any client information after transaction completion. Each transaction is considered as an atomic entity where the server doesn't remember previous transactions. This characteristic makes stateless servers free from crashes as they do not need to maintain any specific state. NFS is a classic example of stateless servers.

On the other hand, in Stateful DFS, servers retain information about the preceding transactions which help in offering more complex services. AFS and Coda are examples of stateful servers.

3.5. Pros and Cons of Distributed File Systems

Distributed File Systems comes with its own set of advantages and disadvantages. On one hand, they ensure high data availability, provide sharing and collaboration facilities and are easily scalable. They also offer redundancy, better data management, and organization, with the added benefit of load balancing. On the contrary, issues like network latency, security concerns, the complexity of setup, and management along with a dependency on stable network connections are some challenges DFS pose.

3.6. Security in Distributed File Systems

Security is a prominent concern in distributed file systems. Primarily, it involves three main aspects: Authentication of users and servers, Authorization of access to files and services, and Ensuring the privacy of data transmitted over the DFS. Authentication verifies the identity of users and machines, Authorization validates access rights, while privacy emphasizes data integrity and confidentiality during transmission.

3.7. Conclusion

The architectural overview captures the essence of Distributed File Systems and its integral components. Understanding these concepts serves a foundational role in optimizing Network File Systems, thereby facilitating better data management and storage. It stands essential, however, to consider its benefits and challenges before implementation. In the succeeding sections, we will narrow down our focus on one such DFS, the NFS, and how its techniques can be optimized for better performance. Stay tuned as we unravel these intricacies in the advanced stages of this report.

Chapter 4. Demystifying NFS Protocols and Procedures

Understanding NFS Protocols and Procedures can be quite a labyrinth to navigate. In this segment, we'll shed light on the associated protocols, their operations, performance implications, and how to tune them for optimal performance.

4.1. Understanding NFS

Originating as part of Sun Microsystem's Network Computing Architecture, NFS is a distributed filesystem protocol that permits a user on a client machine to access files over a network in the same way they would access a local storage file. It does this by enabling file sharing among multiple systems, creating a collaborative working environment.

NFS relies on the Remote Procedure Call (RPC) model that utilizes the client-server communication model. Requests are made by the client, with the server pooling resources to fulfill the request. NFS operations are usually stateless – the server retains no information (state) about the client once the request is processed.

4.2. NFS Versions

The evolution of NFS along with its variations have played a critical role in optimizing distributed file systems.

4.2.1. NFSv2

NFSv2, the first public version, operated statelessly with a stunted 2GB file size limit and featured primitive error recovery mechanisms. All its operations were synchronous, blocking server response until the operation was completed, which often led to slower data access speeds.

4.2.2. NFSv3

NFSv3 was a significant improvement over its predecessor, supporting larger file sizes and introducing asynchronous writes. Clients can send additional write requests without waiting for confirmation of the previous write operation's completion. This leads to improved data throughput rates.

4.2.3. NFSv4

NFSv4 introduces statefulness to the vast operations it supports, including delegated operations which permit a client to make decisions locally, reducing the request-response overhead. Stronger security through Kerberos, easier firewall configuration, and more efficient over-the-network operations get bundled into NFSv4.

4.3. NFS Operations

Inherent to NFS is an array of operations that facilitate the functioning of the protocol. Let's walk through the major operations unique to each NFS version.

4.3.1. NFSv2 and NFSv3 Operations

NFSv2 and NFSv3 primarily support operations like READ, WRITE, CREATE, REMOVE, RENAME, among others. For example, with the READ operation, the client sends the file handle, read offset, and the number of bytes to read. The server then responds with the requested data.

4.3.2. NFSv4 Operations

NFSv4 has consolidated much of the operations into a compound procedure structure that reduces the number of round-trip exchanges between the client and the server. Consequently, this eliminates latency for multiple operations.

4.4. Performance Implications

Despite asynchronous operations in NFSv3 and significant improvements in NFSv4, NFS can still inhibit high-speed network utilization because of latency and the overheads of NFS request conversion into file system operations.

Understanding specific operations and their performance implications are key to optimizing NFS. For instance, READ, performed more frequently than WRITE in most environments, can suffer from network round trip time. The effects can be mitigated by using a larger read size.

4.5. Tuning NFS for Performance

Optimal NFS performance depends on appropriate tuning of parameters. Below are a few strategies:

4.5.1. Server Tuning

1. Adjust `nfsv4.1-server.max-cb-path-down` parameter on Linux servers to allow more callbacks for delegations in NFSv4.

2. Tune the filesystem where files are served from, as much of NFS's performance is tied to the underlying filesystem.

4.5.2. Client Tuning

1. Adjust the `nfs.Client.Timeout` to increase the server response wait time before client retransmission.

2. Enable `nfs.nfsiod` threads to allow asynchronous NFS operations.

4.6. Monitoring NFS

Good comprehension of NFS procedures and performance isn't complete without the instrumentation to monitor it.

4.6.1. Export List

A comprehensive review of the servers' exported directories can be done using the `showmount -e` command.

4.6.2. nfsstat

`nfsstat` is a utility to monitor NFS calls for individual operations. `nfsstat -c` will display client stats, and `nfsstat -s` will display server stats.

4.6.3. /proc Filesystem

For Linux operating machines, the /proc filesystem provides a wealth of statistical information. A common path `/proc/net/rpc/nfsd` provides metrics about the NFS server.

Every intricate element of NFS, its protocols, procedures, variants, and accompanying considerations propels the potential of distributed file systems. In-depth knowledge, the right tools, and consistent monitoring will lead to the successful and optimal use of NFS. With what we've unwrapped thus far, we hope to have demystified the complexities around NFS protocols and procedures.

In the next chapter, we will delve into the finer aspects of NFS Mount Options, which form the crux of fine-tuning your server's performance.

Chapter 5. Advanced NFS Configuration Techniques

The configuration of Network File System (NFS) is a nuanced process, involving a fine balance of numerous variables to achieve optimal efficiency. Employing advanced techniques can lead to a significant performance increase, providing improved accessibility, bandwidth utilization, and availability.

5.1. Understanding NFS performance

Before diving into the specifics of NFS configuration, it's crucial to understand the foundations of NFS performance and the factors that influence it. NFS performance primarily depends on network latency, server and client CPU speeds, the sizes of the read and write requests, as well as the number of network interfaces involved in the process.

In essence, a delay in any of these aspects can reduce the effectiveness of NFS, thereby optimizing these metrics can have a substantial impact. That said, a good understanding of NFS synchronous and asynchronous operations is required for configuration. A server using synchronous operations performs slowly, as it waits for each operation to finish before commencing another, while an asynchronous operation involves multitasking, improving overall performance.

5.2. Configuring NFS for performance optimization

The following advanced techniques contribute to enhancing NFS's performance:

5.2.1. Adjusting the read and write chunk size

The chunk size specifies the maximum amount of data that can be sent in a single read or write request. By adjusting the read and write chunk sizes, you can better optimize the NFS operations to suit your requirements. For incredibly large files, increasing the chunk size can speed up transfers by requiring fewer network packets.

5.3. Use of NFS mount options

A critical approach to NFS configuration involves the use of NFS mount options. Here are some key options you can configure:

- Read/Write Size (`rsize` and `wsize`): These options determine the amount of data that NFS transfers per request. You can adjust these settings to improve NFS performance in data-intensive applications.

- Number of mount retries (`retrans`): This influences the behavior of NFS when facing issues like temporary network outages. Increasing this value ensures that NFS continues attempting to re-establish the connection rather than giving up too soon.

- Timeout value (`timeo`): This option defines how long NFS waits before retransmitting a request. By fine-tuning this value, you can have greater control over your system's performance.

5.4. Configuring NFS for server-side optimization

If you're managing an NFS server, you can apply the following advanced techniques to optimize performance.

5.4.1. Using NFSv4

NFSv4 is the latest version of NFS, offering several enhancements over preceding versions. Going for NFSv4 can result in better performance due to its ability to handle some operations simultaneously, among other advanced features.

5.4.2. Implementing NFS over RDMA

Implementing Remote Direct Memory Access (RDMA) over NFS can lead to enhanced throughput and lesser CPU utilization. NFS over RDMA provides direct access from the memory of one computer to that of another without involving the operating system, thereby increasing the data transfer speed.

5.4.3. Configuring NFS server threads

A server's ability to handle multiple NFS requests simultaneously primarily depends on the number of server threads. Optimizing the number of NFS server threads can significantly improve NFS server performance. Too few threads may cause the server to become bottlenecked with requests while too many might exhaust system resources.

5.5. Fine-tuning NFS for client-side optimization

If you're an NFS client, here are key steps to optimize your operations.

5.5.1. Leveraging the NFS Client Cache

The NFS Client Cache enhances performance by storing data from recent read and write operations. Subsequent requests for the same data can be served from the cache, reducing network traffic and latency.

5.5.2. Implementing Autofs

Autofs is a program that automatically mounts directories when needed and unmounts them after a period of inactivity. Using Autofs with NFS can improve performance by lessening the load on the network.

In conclusion, advanced configuration of NFS is all about making the right system-level decisions that bring together the various pieces of NFS in a way that optimizes performance. Recognize the strengths, weaknesses, and suitable applications of NFS to achieve effective results, and remember that an effective NFS fallback plan is essential to maintaining availability and data integrity in all conditions. Whichever unique challenges or objectives you may face, these techniques will be a valuable tool in your NFS management arsenal.

Chapter 6. Optimizing NFS Performance

Optimizing a Network File System (NFS) isn't just about ticking boxes on a list. It requires a deep understanding of how systems interact, network behavior, and variables that can impact overall performance. This document aims to help users fine-tune their NFS systems, addressing common challenges and providing insights on specific tools that enhance performance.

6.1. Understanding NFS Protocol Versions

There have been four major iterations of NFS since its inception, each refining and expanding upon previous versions. NFSv4, the most recent iteration, introduces stateful operations and better access control management, improvements upon the stateless design of earlier versions, but comes with an added load. Understanding your organization's needs and the trade-offs of each version is essential when optimizing NFS performance.

Verifying the protocol version can be as simple as running the command: `rpcinfo -p`. This operation will reveal which protocol versions are running.

6.2. Optimizing NFS Requests

Network request optimization can massively enhance NFS performance. By discerning the difference between `read ahead` and `write behind` techniques, organizations can manage heavy traffic loads while maintaining high performance.

Read ahead is a methodology where the client predicts which data is required next and then preemptively fetches it. This technique can significantly speed up throughput for large, sequential reads. Conversely, the write behind method involves the client queuing write requests and sending them in bulk, which can reduce overhead for small, random writes.

These techniques can be manipulated through system control using the `sysctl` command, specifically: `vfs.read_max` and `vfs.write_max`.

6.3. Tuning NFS Threads

Dedicating a greater number of kernel threads to NFS helps to distribute and manage the load more efficiently, enhancing performance. The default number of threads is eight per server, but this can be increased via the `nfsd` command under `/etc/sysconfig/nfs`.

Increasing server threads should be implemented cautiously, as there could be potential disruption to service. A sudden influx of threads can flood the system and cause deterioration in performance instead of improvement.

6.4. Leveraging Jumbo Frames

Jumbo Frames is a technique that involves increasing the Maximum Transmission Unit (MTU) size of your Ethernet frames - the smaller pieces into which your data is divided for transmission. The standard MTU size is usually 1500 bytes, but Jumbo Frames allows this to be increased up to 9000 bytes, thereby reducing overhead and improving performance.

However, using Jumbo Frames needs careful consideration. All devices in the network path must support and be configured to use the larger size; misconfiguration will lead to severe transmission issues.

6.5. NFS Client and Server Communication

The relationship between the NFS client and server directly impacts NFS performance. The `rsize` and `wsize` mounted options, which regulate the amount of data a client can read from or write to the server in a single operation, play a significant role in this communication.

By default, these parameters are set to the maximum value supported by both the client and server. However, for the sake of optimization, it could prove beneficial to adjust these settings. A general rule of thumb involves increasing `rsize` for read-heavy workloads and increasing `wsize` for write-heavy workloads - though, of course, specifics will vary depending on individual network and organizational context.

6.6. Addressing Common Problems

Common impediments to optimization need addressing to ensure the smooth operation of your NFS. Alongside more prominent concerns like network issues and hardware malfunctions, minor issues such as small data blocks and time synchronization discrepancies can negatively impact performance.

Small blocks can lead to overpopulation of NFS directory inode caches, hampering effective data management. Increasing the block size can help mitigate this problem. Additionally, discrepancies in time between client and server can cause significant issues with file locking, authentication, and file timestamps. Ensuring both are synchronized can greatly enhance NFS performance.

6.7. Optimizing NFS with SSDs

NFS performance can see a significant boost by employing Solid State Drives (SSDs). Unlike traditional hard drives, SSDs don't have mechanical parts, meaning they're faster and more reliable. SSDs can also handle input/output operations more efficiently, making them a cut above other storage devices and a significant advantage when fine-tuning NFS performance.

In conclusion, optimising NFS performance is an iterative, deeply technical process that requires understanding, tact and patience. By implementing these strategies and tips, you can better navigate the labyrinth of NFS, bolstering your organisation's digital infrastructure and ensuring optimal performance.

Chapter 7. Management of NFS Services

Being a critical and complex component of distributed systems, NFS services require proficient management techniques to ensure their smooth functioning. NFS services management includes service configuration, allocation of resources, security setup and maintenance, the planning and monitoring of performance, and establishing backup and recovery procedures.

7.1. NFS Service Configuration

NFS service configuration involves setting up the NFS server and clients. On the server side, you need to specify which directories to share and the corresponding access permissions. Conversely, on the client side, you need to mount the shared directories from the server. Executing these operations manually can become cumbersome with many NFS servers and clients, so consider using an automation tool like Ansible for this task.

Starting from version 4, NFS also supports pseudo file systems, which allow administrators to represent multiple exported directories from the server as a single tree structure bonded to the client.

7.2. Resource Allocation and Load Balancing

Effective management of NFS services obliges efficient use of resources. It primarily involves determining the appropriate amount of system resources to allot to NFS operations to optimize performance without exhausting the resources of your system.

One approach is to consider load balancing, which can help

distribute network traffic and system utilization evenly across multiple servers. This technique can greatly enhance performance by not overwhelming a single server with all requests. Tools like the IPVS (IP Virtual Server) can aid in instating this capability easily.

7.3. Security Setup and Maintenance

Security in NFS services is paramount to preventing unauthorized access and data breaches. NFS offers several security features like Kerberos for authentication and RPCSEC_GSS for both authentication and encryption. Utilizing these features effectively can provide a secure environment for data sharing.

It is recommended to always keep the software up-to-date to benefit from the latest security fixes and enhancements. Regular audits of NFS-related events can also help to swiftly identify and remediate potential security threats.

7.4. Performance Monitoring and Optimization

Monitoring the performance of NFS services allows administrators to identify bottlenecks and implement optimization strategies timely. Tools such as nfsiostat and Collectl offer insights into NFS I/O statistics, helping ascertain performance attributes.

It's essential to understand that performance optimization is not solely about reacting when issues occur. Rather, it entails proactively employing strategies that maximize performance. Techniques include making use of NFS features like Read Ahead and Write Behind, which help to buffer data and reduce the number of network operations.

7.5. Backup and Recovery Procedures

Establishing reliable backup and recovery procedures is crucial to prevent data loss in adverse circumstances such as hardware failure or accidental deletion. NFS services can be backed up using standard file backup tools.

A suitable disaster recovery plan, on the other hand, ensures minimal service disruption in the face of catastrophic incidents. Such a plan might involve having a redundant secondary server, ready to take over the moment the primary experiences difficulties.

Taking a holistic view, the management of NFS services should be an ongoing operational work encompassing service configuration, resource allocation, security setup, performance monitoring, and backup procedures. As the digital world continues to grow, the need for efficient and secure distributed systems becomes increasingly critical. Through the appropriate and comprehensive management of NFS services, it is indeed attainable to optimize system performance whilst maintaining security and reliability.

Chapter 8. Troubleshooting Common NFS Issues

In any well-architected NFS environment, addressing the common issues is key to ensuring optimal performance and stability. This chapter provides you with an overview of the frequent challenges associated with NFS, along with practical solutions to mitigate them.

8.1. NFS Server Unreachability

The availability of the NFS server directly influences the operation of NFS clients. If a server becomes unreachable, clients lose access to their shared resources. To troubleshoot this issue, consider the following approaches:

1. Test network connectivity: Use the 'ping' or 'traceroute' commands to determine if the network path to the server is clear.

2. Verify NFS Service: Ensure that the NFS server service is active and running correctly. Use the 'rpcinfo' command to verify the NFS services.

3. Check Firewall Rules: Confirm that the NFS ports are open in both the client and server firewall settings. Use the 'iptables' command for checking these rules.

8.2. Mount Point Failures

In some cases, NFS clients may face issues when trying to mount shared directories from the NFS server. A list of tips for troubleshooting mount point failures includes:

1. Check Mount Permissions: Verify that the client IP address has the necessary permissions in the server's '/etc/exports' file.

2. Test RPC Services: Ensure that the necessary RPC services are running on both the server and the client.

8.3. Permission Denied Error

NFS clients might encounter 'Permission Denied' errors while trying to access files and directories. Investigate these errors by examining:

1. User ID (UID) and Group ID (GID): If the mounted directory's UID and GID values do not match between the server and client, access to files and directories will be denied. The 'id' command allows checking these values.

2. Exported Directories: Evaluate the permissions for directories shared on the NFS server. Use the 'exportfs' command to observe these permissions.

8.4. Encountering Slow Performance

Slow performance in NFS can lead to frustration. There can be many root causes behind this including network bottlenecks, server issues, or client complications.

1. Assess Network Speed: Use 'nfsstat' and 'iperf' commands to measure network performance.

2. Review Server Load: High server load can be a cause for slow performance. Commands like 'top', 'vmstat', and 'iostat' can help monitor your server.

3. Increase NFS I/O Size: Tweaking the 'rsize' and 'wsize' NFS options affect the chunk of data NFS handles per operation.

8.5. NFS Lock Issues

In some cases, NFS clients may encounter problems when attempting to lock files, and this can be due to application-level or NFS protocol-level issues.

1. Test lockd Service: Ensure the NFS lock daemon (lockd) is running on both the server and client.

2. Check statd Service: The Network Status Monitor (statd) works alongside lockd for crash and recovery operations. Statd's running status and configuration should be checked if any NFS lock issues are encountered.

3. Examine Application-Level Locks: Some applications don't work well with NFS lock management and will need careful configuration.

Troubleshooting NFS issues may become an ongoing process in your role as a network administrator. This guide provides you with a starting point for resolving some of the most common challenges you might encounter. The important part is to be systematic and thoughtful in your approach while not losing sight of the bigger picture: a stable, secure, and performant NFS setup.

Chapter 9. NFS Security Best Practices

NFS security is crucial in modern distributed environments. By implementing best security practices, you are safeguarding your systems and data against unauthorized access, tampering, and harmful intent. This comprehensive section will explore the various methods to secure your NFS correctly.

9.1. Client And Server Security

The first line of defense in an NFS setup should be securing the client and server systems. Keep all systems up to date with the latest security patches. Regular updating ensures you are protected from known vulnerabilities that could be exploited. For additional security, utilize intrusion detection systems (IDS) and firewalls. IDS helps detect any unauthorized access attempts, and firewalls restrict access to your systems.

9.2. User Access Control

Both the client and server operations associated with NFS are based on the user's identity, the user's group, and the user's access privileges. User-level security is crucial. It enables the system to differentiate between different users and appropriately allocate their access rights. NFS uses traditional Unix-style access controls, such as user and group IDs and file permissions.

- Use the root_squash option: This option maps the root user UID and GID from the client side to anonymous user IDs on the Server side. Hence, even if a root user attempts to access files, the actions are restricted based on the anonymity credentials.

- Allowing trusted users: You can specify trusted users to have unrestricted access by setting the no_root_squash option. This option grants root user requests the same permissions as the root user on the server side. Using this option, be aware of potential security risks.

- Using all_squash option: This option forces all client requests to be treated as anonymous, regardless of the actual UID and GID from the client side.

9.3. Secure NFS

NFS version 4 introduced 'secure NFS' where security is integrated into the protocol: Kerberos support provides authentication, integrity, and confidentiality, ensuring your data remains secured. Kerberos is a network authentication protocol that verifies the identities of clients and servers to establish secure connections.

Kerberos security strategy consists of:

- krb5: Ensures that the data transfer between the NFS client and server is authenticated but not encrypted.

- krb5i: A step above krb5, it also ensures integrity. The data isn't just authenticated; it's also checked for any tampering during transfer.

- krb5p: The most secure mode, krb5p brings confidentiality into the picture. The data is not only authenticated and checked for integrity, but it's also encrypted to ensure confidentiality of the data in transfer.

9.4. Firewall Considerations

Firewalls are an essential aspect of server security. However, configuring firewalls for NFS can be challenging due to the use of Remote Procedure Call (RPC) by NFS. Administrators need time to understand the intricacies involved.

- One approach is to run an NFS firewall with static ports. The administrator manually specifies the port numbers that NFS uses for its services.

- On the other hand, using a firewall with RPC might require more configuration efforts. RPC calls are difficult to predict since the ports are dynamically allocated, but using firewalld and rpcbind can quell this issue.

9.5. Export Control

Export control defines what part of the local file system an NFS server exports to remote clients. Correct configuration of export controls significantly influences the security of the system.

- Be as restrictive as possible: Only export directories that clients need to access and only to known and trusted clients.

- Use the ro option: The 'ro' or read-only option allows clients to only read files from the directory and not write or modify them. This safeguards the data against unauthorized modifications.

- Use the sync option: This ensures that changes to files are immediately flushed to disk. By setting sync, you ensure that the file system remains consistent even during an unexpected crash.

NFS security is vital in the world of distributed file systems. This guide offers some best practice approaches to secure your data and systems effectively. In conclusion, remember to stay vigilant; security is a process that needs constant updates and tweaking based on the latest threats and technological advancements. Indeed, maintaining secure NFS is not an event but an ongoing journey of vigilance and knowledge application.

Chapter 10. Case Studies: Real-world Applications of NFS

Whether we acknowledge it or not, the Network File System (NFS) forms an integral part of our world's digital tapestry, streamlining countless processes across sundry industries. It's only fitting, therefore, that we delve deep into concrete applications of Amazon FSx for Windows and Linux, the client-server file sharing protocol, NFS, and the VMware vSphere.

10.1. Harnessing NFS in the Genome Sequencing Industry

Bioinformatics relies heavily on large datasets. Compute nodes use significant I/O capacity to profile genomes, so high-performance is essential for processing data. Enter NFS, unlocking unparalleled data sharing and accessibility in an otherwise resource-intensive sector.

A leading genome processing company instituted NFSv4.1 to manage substantial data volumes between hundreds of compute nodes. PVC (Persistent Volume Claim) access modes standardized ReadWriteMany operations. In short, NFS served as a bioinformatics-friendly file system, enabling data access, consistency, and security.

10.2. University Libraries Leverage NFS

In the realm of academia, NFS supports library computer systems that often house extensive databases. A university library system introduced NFS3 to enable uninterrupted access to countless e-books, research papers, theses, and other reference materials. By connecting the participating library servers to an NFS-based system, the articles and books became easily accessible across student and faculty devices with zero latency. Query performance and data integrity improved, effectively turning the tide on heavy traffic during peak academic periods.

10.3. Optimizing Media Companies with NFS

The media industry demands continuous, real-time access to massive digital libraries. Media conglomerates engage NFS to centralize storage systems and ensure consistent access from multiple nodes concurrently, negating the need for individual data copies.

A renowned media company transitioned to NFS to manage its digital assets. The seamless integration allowed graphic artists, video editors, and other users to work in unison, despite differing geographic locations. NFS reduced data redundancy, improved collaboration, and catalyzed project completion.

10.4. NFS in Manufacturing Industry

Modern manufacturing plants demand sophisticated solutions to manage and process significant data quantities. A prominent automation company introduced NFSv4.1 to ensure concurrent and consistent file sharing. With its stateful architecture, it offered a secure, lock management facility for essential CAD files.

The result was a reduction in data redundancy and improved protection against data losses that could arise from unexpected outages. Thus, NFS bolstered its importance in just-in-time manufacturing environments.

10.5. NFS and the Telecommunications Industry

The telecommunications industry—with its vast data sets—often struggles to manage, secure, and analyze its data efficiently. A global telecom enterprise introduced NFS to handle such big data.

NFS permitted rapid file transfers between multiple servers, ensuring agility and minimum downtime. Distributed servers implemented simultaneous operations to offload traffic from central servers. With NFS, the enterprise reduced read/write times and succeeded in delivering an enhanced user experience.

Summing up these case studies, NFS indeed revolutionizes multiple sectors with its high-performance file sharing capabilities. In a world grappling with the complexities of distributed systems, mastering NFS techniques can pave the way for an optimized, streamlined future. The network's capacity for consistent, secure, and efficient data management has already transformed numerous real-world systems, signifying its critical role in the digital age.

The exploration doesn't stop here. Taking these proven applications, we can glean vital pointers on implementing NFS in diverse scenarios. Applying these experiences and lessons when optimizing distributed file systems can not only prevent potential pitfalls but can also significantly enhance the overall system performance. We continue onto the final sections of this report, equipped with a better understanding of NFS's capabilities. In the coming sections, we will delve deeper into NFS management, potential challenges and, of course, how to overcome them.

Chapter 11. Future Outlook: NFS and Cloud-based File Systems

In light of the constant evolution of technology, the expectations for Network File System (NFS) are dynamic and progressively expanding. These evolving needs demand innovations in storage solutions, specifically relating to aspects of robustness, resilience, and accessibility. NFS has fit the bill thus far. However, the increasing shift towards cloud-based file systems offers exciting possibilities for the future.

11.1. NFS: Streams of Evolution

NFS made its first appearance in 1984, providing a client-server protocol for file sharing over a network. With the advent of NFS v4, many improvements have been realized, such as better security features, efficient WAN operation, and support for file locking and mounting. Today, the NFS protocol has become the de facto standard for file sharing on UNIX and Linux systems and is progressively gaining ground in other spaces.

While NFS has come a long way, it is not immune to the pressures of changing technological landscapes. The digital world is marked by an outpouring of massive volume of data, demanding ever-more-efficient systems for data management and storage. Responding to these pressures, NFS has sought to evolve through versions and enhancements, all while retaining its simplicity and effectiveness.

One instance of such evolution is parallel NFS (pNFS), a part of NFS v4.1, which allows clients to access storage devices directly and in parallel. This translates to improved bandwidth, flexibility, and scalability, greatly optimizing the overall performance.

11.2. Cloud-based File Systems: An Emerging Trend

However, the rapidly growing cloud-based technology wave presents an inevitable disruption. Cloud-based file systems, the latest breakthrough in data storage technology, provide scalable, robust, and distributed storage that's accessible from literally anywhere, offering a new dimension to how we interact with data.

The allure of cloud-based systems is appealing, with attributes like scalability, data integrity, high availability, and cost efficiency topping the list of desirables. These systems offer virtually unlimited storage space, eliminating the physical constraints of conventional storage. Coupling this with effortless data retrieval and high resilience against data loss, the shift hardly comes as a surprise.

Furthermore, with a pay-as-you-use model, organizations can cut down significantly on upfront investments in storage infrastructure. The cloud also offers a range of disaster recovery solutions, ensuring organizations' data is safe and redundantly stored.

11.3. NFS and Cloud-based File Systems: The Intersection

While we marvel at these advances in cloud technology, the question that arises is - What does this mean for NFS?

Rather than considering cloud-based file systems as an outright replacement for NFS, we should consider how the strengths of both could intersect to create more efficient data management systems.

Currently, coupling NFS with cloud technology is already changing how we approach data management and storage. Cloud NFS or cloud-based NFS services, such as Amazon's EFS and Google's Cloud

Filestore, provide fully managed file systems that can be accessed by multiple instances and applications. These cloud-based NFS services blend the traditional benefits of NFS with the scalability and flexibility of cloud architecture.

The integration of NFS with cloud technology allows enterprises to build and operate scalable infrastructure for data management with less complexity. By relievably distributing file systems across multiple locations, these enterprises guarantee streamlined operations, improved performance, and reduced cost.

11.4. The Prospects of NFS in Hybrid Cloud Environments

The next logical step for the convergence of NFS and cloud is the hybrid cloud environment. This setup would allow enterprises to gain from the scalability and cost-efficiency benefits of the cloud without entirely forsaking existing on-premise NFS infrastructure. By harnessing both on-premise and cloud storage, hybrid environments deliver flexibility and control, which is a valuable proposition for businesses with dynamic data storage requirements.

Multiple tech giants are proposing solutions for this, such as Microsoft's Azure NetApp Files, a high-performance file storage service. It supports migration of enterprise NFS workloads to Azure and is integrated with Azure's other services, providing a comprehensive method to meet on-premise and cloud storage requirements.

11.5. Bumps on the Road Ahead

Despite the promising outlook, there are challenges to overcome. These include provisioning and de-provisioning storage, latency issues, managing and scheduling resources, and ensuring data security and privacy, which can be complex in a cloud environment.

Moreover, the cloud's pay-as-you-go model, although economically attractive, can also lead to cost inefficiencies if not managed properly. The dynamic feature of cloud storage requires continuous monitoring and intelligent management to prevent unnecessary expenses.

11.6. Final Thoughts

In conclusion, the advancements in cloud-based file systems, coupled with the enduring and versatile nature of NFS, promises an exciting future. NFS is set to evolve beyond local networks and servers to cloud networks, creating a hybrid storage solution that captivates the best of both worlds. Nevertheless, we must acknowledge and address the challenges that lie ahead, for which ongoing research and investment into the field is essential.

The dialogue around NFS and cloud storage is only beginning. As technology progresses, the potential for improvements, adjustments, and refinements in the conversation arise. As part of this progression, we anticipate an increasingly seamless integration of distributed file systems with other advanced technologies, such as machine learning and IoT, which could change the very way we perceive and interact with data. The future brings endless possibilities, and we look forward to seeing what lies in store for NFS and cloud-based file systems.

9 798885 622541 8